HUGE ART

James Driver

OXFORD

UNIVERSITY PRESS

Contents

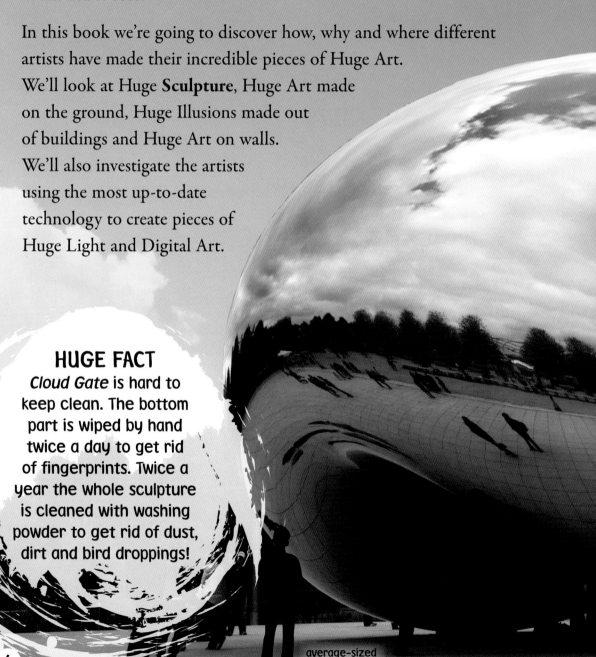

What is Huge Art?

Huge Art is amazing. It makes you stop and wonder. Who thought of that? How did they make it so big? Why did they make it so big? What did it cost?

In this book we're going to discover how, why and where different artists have made their incredible pieces of Huge Art. We'll look at Huge **Sculpture**, Huge Art made on the ground, Huge Illusions made out of buildings and Huge Art on walls. We'll also investigate the artists using the most up-to-date technology to create pieces of Huge Light and Digital Art.

HUGE FACT

Cloud Gate is hard to keep clean. The bottom part is wiped by hand twice a day to get rid of fingerprints. Twice a year the whole sculpture is cleaned with washing powder to get rid of dust, dirt and bird droppings!

average-sized human being

This is *Cloud Gate* by Anish Kapoor. It is in Millennium Park in Chicago, USA. Because it is made of shiny **stainless steel** it reflects the buildings all around it, and a huge area of the ever-changing sky above. It looks different every time you see it.

Cloud Gate is visited by hundreds of thousands of people every year. Because it is so big it is easy for everyone in a large crowd to see it, touch it, walk around it and feel they are part of it.

This is

HUGE ART.

Huge Sculpture

Boy by Ron Mueck

It is really surprising to see something that is much, much bigger than we expect it to be. Ron Mueck's *Boy* is many times larger than he would be in real life. Everything about him, including his hair, his skin, his clothing, his eyes and his toenails, is completely lifelike.

Look at the size of the **sculptor** compared to the size of *Boy*. Making something much bigger changes the way we think about it and prompts us to ask questions.

Why do you think *Boy* is covering his face?

What do you think the sculptor is thinking?

What do you think *Boy* is thinking?

What is *Boy* made of?

Boy is mainly made out of **fibreglass**. Ron Mueck also uses natural materials like horsehair. Once he used his own hair to make one of his sculptures as realistic as possible.

Mueck's huge pieces of art make us feel as if we are scientists looking at strange creatures through a magnifying glass. They make us think harder about ourselves.

HUGE FACT
Boy took eight months to make, is almost five metres tall and weighs around 500 kilograms.

About the artist
Before he became a sculptor, Ron Mueck made puppets for children's television and films. As well as making some of the models and masks for the 1986 film *Labyrinth*, he also operated the puppet and provided the voice of the friendly monster, Ludo.

Mount Rushmore and Crazy Horse

average-sized human being

It's hard to miss sculpture that is carved out of a mountain! This is Mount Rushmore. The giant heads are cut out of solid **granite**. They are the faces of four famous American presidents. Mount Rushmore is one of the most visited places in the USA, with almost three million tourists coming to see it every year.

George Washington

Thomas Jefferson

Theodore Roosevelt

Abraham Lincoln

	Mount Rushmore	Crazy Horse Memorial
Started	1927	1948
Finished	1941	Still being carved
Subject	Four American presidents	A Lakota chief on his horse
Method	Explosives and power hammers	Explosives, power hammers and jet flames
Height of heads	18 metres	27 metres
Rock removed	450 000 tonnes	Over 7 000 000 tonnes, so far
Paid for by	The US government	Members of the public
Sculptors	Borglum family	Ziolkowski family

Mount Rushmore is right in the middle of the land where the Lakota people, a Native American tribe, once lived. Some of their **descendants** are creating a huge sculpture of Lakota chief Crazy Horse. This memorial is being carved out of another mountain less than 14 kilometres away from Mount Rushmore.

average-sized
human being

HUGE FACT
When it is finished, the Crazy Horse Memorial will be the biggest sculpture in the world.

We are the Lakota people. The American government took our land from us. Crazy Horse was one of our greatest leaders and he led us in a bitter war against the American government. We helped to win the Battle of the Little Bighorn in 1876.

Field by Antony Gormley

Not all Huge Sculptures come in one piece. *Field* was the idea of
the famous sculptor Antony Gormley, but he didn't make it himself.
Instead, he asked many different people from many different places
to help. To make the British version, Antony Gormley asked for 100
volunteers from two schools near Liverpool. They, and members of
their families, made about 40 000 figures.

Versions of *Field* have been made all over
the world. It has been seen in Mexico,
Brazil, Sweden, China, Japan and
Australia. *Field* is simple and complicated
at the same time. It is simple because it is
made up of thousands and thousands of
small **clay** figures. Each one is between
6 and 8 centimetres high. The figures
have been made so they are similar to
each other, but none are exactly the same.
The same could be said about the people
who made them.

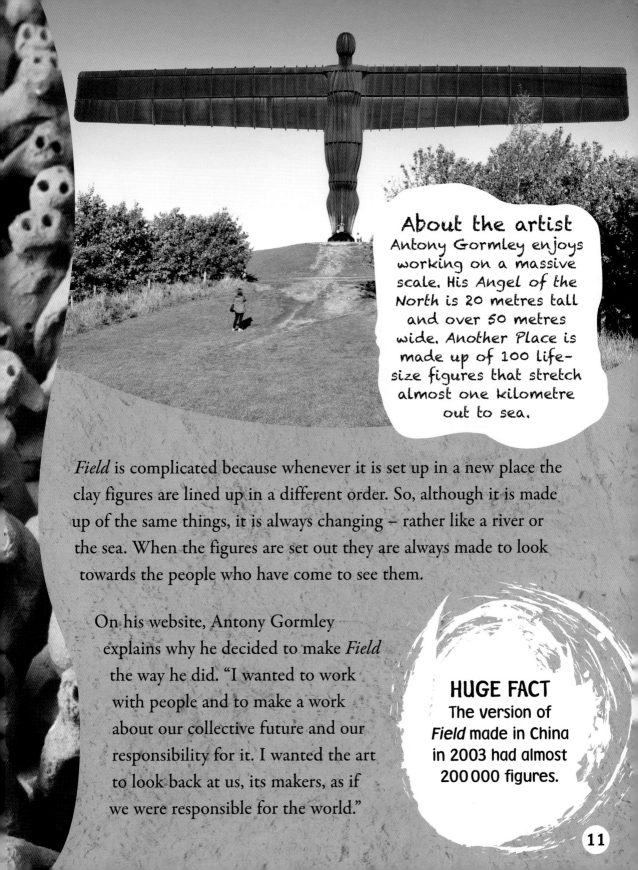

About the artist
Antony Gormley enjoys working on a massive scale. His *Angel of the North* is 20 metres tall and over 50 metres wide. *Another Place* is made up of 100 life-size figures that stretch almost one kilometre out to sea.

Field is complicated because whenever it is set up in a new place the clay figures are lined up in a different order. So, although it is made up of the same things, it is always changing – rather like a river or the sea. When the figures are set out they are always made to look towards the people who have come to see them.

On his website, Antony Gormley explains why he decided to make *Field* the way he did. "I wanted to work with people and to make a work about our collective future and our responsibility for it. I wanted the art to look back at us, its makers, as if we were responsible for the world."

HUGE FACT
The version of *Field* made in China in 2003 had almost 200 000 figures.

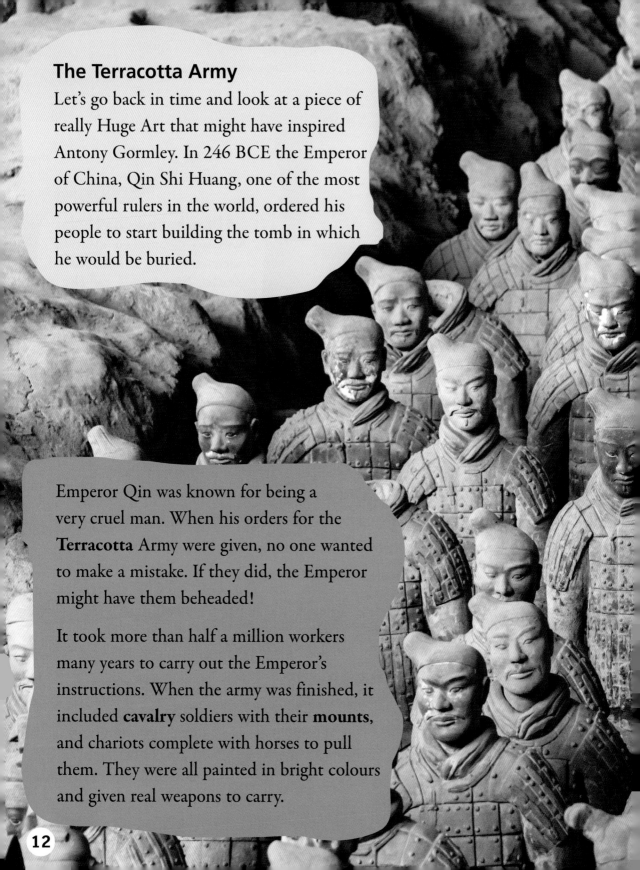

The Terracotta Army

Let's go back in time and look at a piece of really Huge Art that might have inspired Antony Gormley. In 246 BCE the Emperor of China, Qin Shi Huang, one of the most powerful rulers in the world, ordered his people to start building the tomb in which he would be buried.

Emperor Qin was known for being a very cruel man. When his orders for the **Terracotta** Army were given, no one wanted to make a mistake. If they did, the Emperor might have them beheaded!

It took more than half a million workers many years to carry out the Emperor's instructions. When the army was finished, it included **cavalry** soldiers with their **mounts**, and chariots complete with horses to pull them. They were all painted in bright colours and given real weapons to carry.

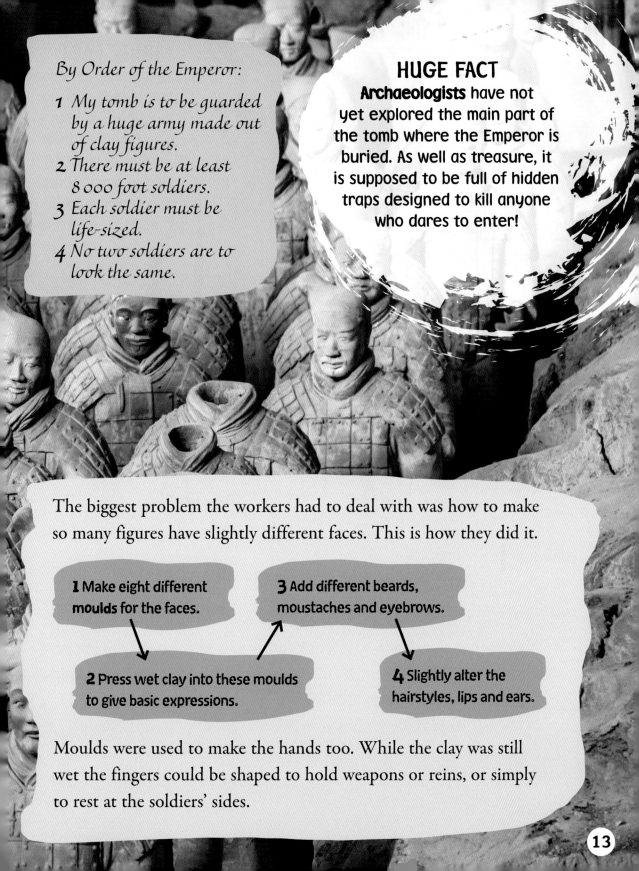

By Order of the Emperor:

1 *My tomb is to be guarded by a huge army made out of clay figures.*
2 *There must be at least 8 000 foot soldiers.*
3 *Each soldier must be life-sized.*
4 *No two soldiers are to look the same.*

HUGE FACT

Archaeologists have not yet explored the main part of the tomb where the Emperor is buried. As well as treasure, it is supposed to be full of hidden traps designed to kill anyone who dares to enter!

The biggest problem the workers had to deal with was how to make so many figures have slightly different faces. This is how they did it.

1 Make eight different **moulds** for the faces.

2 Press wet clay into these moulds to give basic expressions.

3 Add different beards, moustaches and eyebrows.

4 Slightly alter the hairstyles, lips and ears.

Moulds were used to make the hands too. While the clay was still wet the fingers could be shaped to hold weapons or reins, or simply to rest at the soldiers' sides.

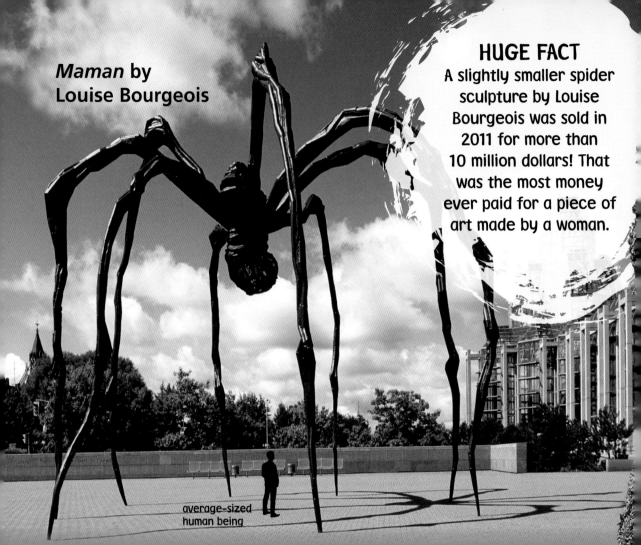

Maman by Louise Bourgeois

average-sized human being

Maman is the French word for mother. When the French artist Louise Bourgeois was asked why she had called her giant spider sculpture _Maman_, she said she had made it in memory of her mother.

Many people find spiders scary. In books and films like _Lord of the Rings_ and _Harry Potter_ they are often shown as dangerous monsters. Bourgeois didn't think so, though. She explained that spiders weave their webs, and her mother had been a weaver too. Because spiders catch flies and mosquitoes they are helpful to us, and this reminded Bourgeois of the many different ways that her mother had cared for her.

Puppy by Jeff Koons

It can be quite hard for us to understand exactly why Louise Bourgeois made a giant metal spider in memory of her mother. It seems much easier to understand what Jeff Koons means when he says that *Puppy* is a piece about "love and happiness".

It's hard to think of anything more comforting than a big, soft, 13-metre-tall puppy made of sweet-smelling flowers!

But *Puppy* is only simple on the surface. Because it is a sculpture made of living things it needs almost as much looking after as a real puppy.

Hidden away inside the sculpture is a steel framework holding over 25 tonnes of soil. A mass of water pipes keeps the earth moist so the plants don't die.

Artworks that seem simple are often the most complicated.

HUGE FACT
Puppy is made up of more than 70 000 separate flowering plants.

average-sized human being

The Kelpies by Andy Scott

Huge Sculpture is often expensive. Sometimes the people who pay for it don't only want it to be exciting art, they often want it to do something useful too.

The Kelpies are two massive horse heads made from stainless steel that have been built near the Forth and Clyde Canal on the east coast of Scotland. Their job is to attract people into the area.

The more visitors who come to this part of Scotland, the more work there will be for the people who live there. It is hoped that *The Kelpies* will make this area of Scotland famous throughout the world.

HUGE FACT
Each kelpie weighs more than 300 tonnes. At 30 metres high, they are Scotland's tallest works of art.

Why horses?

There were several reasons why the sculptures were made to look like horse heads. A kelpie is a mythical Scottish water creature with the strength of ten ordinary horses. Powerful water creatures seemed to fit in with the local canals and waterways. This area of Scotland is also famous for a local breed of horses, the Clydesdale. They are some of the biggest and most powerful horses in the world – just like the sculpture.

About the artist

Andy Scott, the sculptor, had a special reason to make massive horses. His father had lived nearby and could remember how important horses had been in the area. They worked on the farms, hauled wagons for local factories and pulled barges on the canals.

average-sized human being

COME AND MEET THE KELPIES

One of the wonders of 21st century Scotland. For the full story, pop in to our brand new state-of-the-art visitors' centre.

We're easy to find, just off the M9, halfway between Glasgow and Edinburgh.

While you're here, discover how the Forth and Clyde Canal can give you the holiday of a lifetime. Let *The Kelpies* work their magic!

House by Rachel Whiteread

Remember how we looked at *Boy* and were surprised to see something ordinary looking so big? Rachel Whiteread is another sculptor who makes huge pieces of art out of things we see around us every day. By doing something unusual with these common objects she makes us think about them in different ways.

One of Rachel Whiteread's strangest surprises was the piece she called *House* – a house filled with concrete. We are so used to walking from one place to another, up and down stairs, through different rooms and along corridors, we forget how easily we move through everyday spaces.

By turning these areas into something we can never step into, Rachel Whiteread makes us think differently about the spaces that we live in.

average-sized
human being

In an even bigger sculpture called *Embankment,* Whiteread stacked up 14 000 solid shapes made out of white plastic. Each was the exact shape of the space you find inside a cardboard box. For some people, walking between the solid boxes that will never be opened made them think of all the things they hide away during their lives. *Embankment* reminded other people of the last scene in the film *Indiana Jones and the Raiders of the Lost Ark.*

HUGE FACT
In 1993 *House* won Rachel Whiteread the Turner Prize for being the best young British artist.

Huge Land Art

Christo and Jeanne-Claude (for many years they just called themselves 'Christo') were unusual artists who worked on a gigantic scale, wrapping very large objects in fabric. Their artworks took years to plan and involved many people in their making, but usually lasted for only two weeks. When the work was **dismantled**, nothing remained. Very few artists destroy their work when they have finished it!

TITLE	SURROUNDED ISLANDS
WHEN MADE	1983
WHAT AND WHERE	ISLANDS IN FLORIDA
MATERIALS USED	FLOATING FRAMES AND PINK FABRIC
VISITORS	UNKNOWN

TITLE	THE PONT NEUF WRAPPED
WHEN MADE	1985
WHAT AND WHERE	ONE OF THE MOST FAMOUS BRIDGES IN PARIS
MATERIALS USED	40 000 SQUARE METRES OF SAND-COLOURED FABRIC
VISITORS	ABOUT 3 MILLION

Because they used public places, these artists could not charge people to see their work. To make enough money to pay for their next project, they had to sell the drawings and plans they had made for previous projects.

TITLE	WRAPPED REICHSTAG
WHEN MADE	1995
WHAT AND WHERE	THE PARLIAMENT BUILDING IN GERMANY
MATERIALS USED	100 000 SQUARE METRES OF ALUMINIUM FIREPROOF FABRIC, 15 KILOMETRES OF ROPE
VISITORS	ABOUT 5 MILLION

Why cover or surround well-known structures or huge locations like this? Christo and Jeanne-Claude wanted to give people something new and beautiful to look at, and to encourage them to see familiar things in very different ways.

HUGE FACT
Christo and Jeanne-Claude were born on the same day in the same year: 13th June 1935.

TITLE	THE GATES
WHEN MADE	2005
WHAT AND WHERE	OVER 7000 GATEWAYS ALONG THE PATHS OF CENTRAL PARK, NEW YORK
MATERIALS USED	SAFFRON–COLOURED FABRIC AND 96 KILOMETRES OF TUBING
VISITORS	IT IS BELIEVED UP TO 4 MILLION PEOPLE COULD HAVE PASSED THROUGH THE GATES

What object or place would you wrap up to transform it into a piece of Huge Art?

average-sized
human being

Jim Denevan

Jim Denevan makes his art with natural materials like sand, ice and soil.
He often chooses places, like beaches, where the forces of nature will
quickly destroy what he has done. Jim's work is photographed from the
air. If this didn't happen, most people would never be able to see what he
had made. Aerial photos show us just how big his artwork is!

The biggest artwork in the world!

One of Denevan's strangest projects was to try to make the biggest
artwork in the world. He took a team to the remote Lake Baikal in
Siberia, the deepest lake in the world. Armed with snow shovels and
brooms, they cleared the ice from the surface of the frozen lake to create
a huge series of rings. This 'drawing' covered over 14 square kilometres.
When summer came in May, the sun melted the ice. The expedition was
paid for by a company that used the photographs of Denevan's work on
their website.

The Nazca Lines

No one knows why these huge pictures were made over 1500 years ago in the Nazca Desert in Peru.

The monkey in this photograph is 110 metres long! Some archaeologists think the Nazca people believed their gods would like to look down on these pictures in the desert. Others think they look like the shapes of the stars in the night sky. Because the Nazca people did not use writing, we will probably never know for sure.

Like Jim Denevan, the Nazca people made their lines with simple methods. By scraping away the red-brown pebbles that covered the desert floor, they revealed the light-coloured earth beneath. As well as the monkey, there is a dog, a spider, a hummingbird and a **condor**.

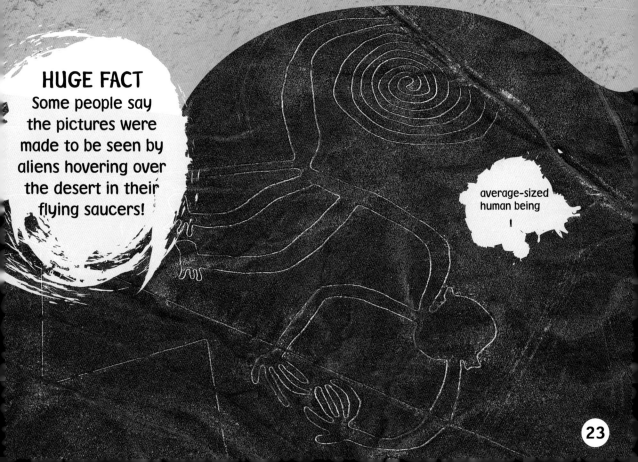

HUGE FACT
Some people say the pictures were made to be seen by aliens hovering over the desert in their flying saucers!

average-sized human being

Wish by Jorge Rodríguez-Gerada

average-sized
human being

HUGE FACT
Jorge Rodríguez-Gerada, who designed *Wish*, was so excited that so many people wanted to help make it, he doubled its size!

WISH FACT FILE

Created: 2013.

Location: Belfast, Northern Ireland

Size: About the same size as six football pitches.

Materials: It is made entirely out of natural materials, mainly sand and soil.

Method: Using GPS (global positioning system) technology, over 30 000 pegs were used to mark out where the lines of soil should be placed. These were then raked into their correct positions by teams of volunteers.

Result: It was the biggest land-art **portrait** ever made in the UK and Ireland.

Seen from the air, or from one of the tall buildings that are nearby, *Wish*'s brown lines look like those in old-fashioned **sepia** photographs. Up close, it is clear that they are long, thin piles of soil laid out in careful lines.

Painted Rocks by Jean Veran

Land artists work mainly with natural materials. Jim Denevan used snow to create his circles. Jorge Rodríguez-Gerada brought in lorry-loads of soil. In a work called *Spiral Jetty*, Robert Smithson moved rocks and earth to create a spiral shape in a lake.

When artists change what has been somewhere for thousands of years, the results can be startling. These rocks in Morocco are thought to have been painted by a mysterious Belgian artist called Jean Veran in 1984. They are known simply as *Painted Rocks*. No one seems to know why Veran chose this spot or these colours. This type of art raises lots of questions and there are no obvious answers.

What might these rocks represent?

What else might look good if it was unexpectedly painted?

Do these painted rocks count as art?

HUGE FACT
Some people believe Veran was helped by Moroccan firefighters who sprayed the paint onto the rocks with their hoses, but the truth remains a mystery.

Huge Wall Art

The Continuous Drawing by Tjebbe van Tijen

In 1967, a Dutch artist called Tjebbe van Tijen had an idea for a piece of really Huge Art. He would draw a line using chalk that went from London to Amsterdam – a journey of about 350 kilometres!

Tjebbe and some friends began the Continuous Drawing outside a famous art gallery, the Institute of Contemporary Art, which is close to Trafalgar Square in London. The police weren't very keen on the idea and washed part of the line away. But Tjebbe and his friends carried on, drawing the line over people, books, newspapers and magazines, as well as walls, pavements and lamp-posts.

While the group was drawing, another one of Tjebbe's friends tried to find a taxi driver who wouldn't mind having his taxi covered in lines. It took some time, but when he finally found one, they were driven to the airport.

At the airport they drew the line all over their luggage, and all over the faces of any passengers who didn't mind!

As soon as Tjebbe and his friends stepped off the plane in Amsterdam they started drawing the line across the floor, onto the airport bus, along the streets of the city, over the walls of an art gallery and in the square outside the Royal Palace.

When the line finally came to an end, Tjebbe was very happy that it had finished its long journey. Most of the people who had seen it go by were left feeling very, very puzzled!

The Great Rubik's Cube™ Mosaic

A mosaic is a picture made from many small, differently coloured pieces of glass, **ceramics** or plastic. These little pieces are called tesserae.

A Rubik's Cube is a puzzle made up of little blocks with different colours on different sides. The Cube Works Studio in Toronto, Canada realized that they could be made to work just like tesserae. In 2013, the studio made the biggest Rubik's Cube mosaic the world had ever seen. It is on the waterfront in the Chinese city of Macau and shows the main buildings of the city. The mosaic is 4 metres tall and more than 60 metres long!

HUGE FACT
The mosaic was made from 85 794 Rubik's Cubes!

average-sized human being

How to make the world's biggest Rubik's Cube Mosaic

1 Take a Rubik's Cube.

2 Turn the blocks until the colours you want are in exactly the right places.

3 Do the same with 80 000 other Rubik's Cubes!

4 Put the Rubik's Cubes together to make your huge mosaic.

The People's Monarch by Helen Marshall

HUGE FACT
The finished mosaic
is the size of a
double-decker bus!

In 2012, the artist Helen Marshall made a huge mosaic
to celebrate the Diamond Jubilee of Queen Elizabeth II.
As you get close to the picture, you can see that it is made
from colour photographs of thousands of people from the
UK. The individual photographs were arranged so that,
when seen from a distance, they blended together to create
a portrait of the Queen.

Huge Digital Art

Face Britain by Ross Ashton

Just like *The People's Monarch,* the artwork *Face Britain* was created in 2012 to celebrate Elizabeth II being Queen of England for 60 years. 201 948 children in the UK uploaded their **self-portraits** onto the *Face Britain* webpage. This was the largest number of artists who had ever worked together on the same artwork, and set a new world record! The portraits were projected as massive digital pictures onto the front of Buckingham Palace in London.

HUGE FACT
The previous world record for the largest number of artists working on the same piece was only 28 267!

Ross Ashton was in charge of projecting *Face Britain* onto Buckingham Palace. He uses huge buildings the way other artists use pieces of paper.

Q: How does Ross choose what to do?
A: First of all he decides what sort of pictures will suit the building. If it's a castle he might choose pictures of knights. For a library he might use huge words, or illustrations from famous books.

Q: What does he do next?
A: He looks closely at the surface of the building. Different materials, like brick and stone, will affect the way the colours will appear. He checks where the windows, doors and other main features are. This helps him decide where to project the different parts of the pictures.

Q: What equipment does he need?
A: He uses projectors that are very powerful – and very expensive! They can send the pictures from up to 150 metres away. Ross will often have several running at once.

Huge Light Art

The Bay Bridge by Leo Villareal

If you pick up an LED (light-emitting diode), it is tiny. Look, this is only 3mm wide! How can something so small make Huge Art?

Putting long strings of LEDs together can produce huge pieces of Light Art. LEDs have become much cheaper and more powerful in the last few years. Because of this, they are being used more often by artists, and on a far bigger scale.

In 2013, the American light artist Leo Villareal attached 25 000 white LEDs to the Bay Bridge in San Francisco. A computer program switched the lights on and off in different patterns. Sometimes it seemed as if the lights were crossing the bridge!

Start small, THINK BIG!

HUGE FACT
The Bay Bridge lights stretched for an amazing 2.9 kilometres and went as high as 160 metres!

Lucid Stead by Phillip K. Smith III

The Californian desert in and around Joshua Tree National Park is a huge, empty place. With hardly any buildings and very few trees you can see a long way in every direction. The skies are often clear, both night and day.

The artist Phillip K. Smith III wanted to try to capture the beautiful way in which the light of the desert slowly changes. Using an old shack and long, thin mirrors, he created this extraordinary building that looks as though you can see straight through it. At night he made it even more magical by programming LEDs to change colour, very slowly, in the windows.

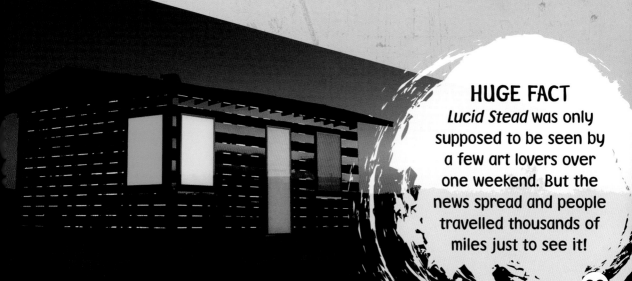

HUGE FACT
Lucid Stead was only supposed to be seen by a few art lovers over one weekend. But the news spread and people travelled thousands of miles just to see it!

Huge Illusions
Dalston House by Leandro Erlich

Leandro Erlich wants us to think about what is and isn't real. At a first glance, it looks like these people are defying gravity by climbing all over the front of a tall building. When you look again, you realize that they are simply standing on a flat surface. They are reflected in a huge overhead mirror and this creates the illusion that they are actually standing on the front of the building.

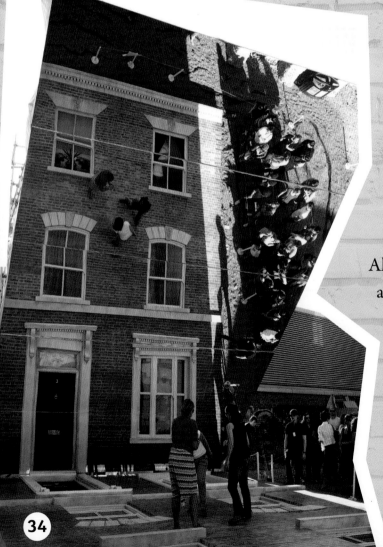

HUGE FACT
Leandro Erlich once made a life-sized swimming pool that allows you to walk under the water completely dry!

Although Leandro Erlich's artwork is fun, it is also making a serious point. He thinks we become so used to extraordinary things – like huge buildings that don't fall down – we are in danger of forgetting how amazing they really are.

From the Knees of my Nose to the Belly of my Toes by Alex Chinneck

Alex Chinneck's huge artworks make passers-by stop, stare and wonder if they can really believe what they are seeing. It looks like the front of this old house has slid down into the front yard.

In the artwork below, it takes a while to realize that this building appears to have been turned completely upside down. Everything – the front door, the windows, the shopfront, even the 'For Sale' sign – is the wrong way up! He gave this artwork another unusual title too: *Miner on the Moon.*

average-sized human being

Alex Chinneck made these illusions by building frameworks of wood and metal and then covering them with thin layers of bricks and other real building materials.

Just like many of the artists in this book, you can be inspired by anything to create Huge Art.

HUGE FACT
Another of Alex Chinneck's ideas was to build a life-sized house out of wax bricks, and then leave it to melt in the sun!

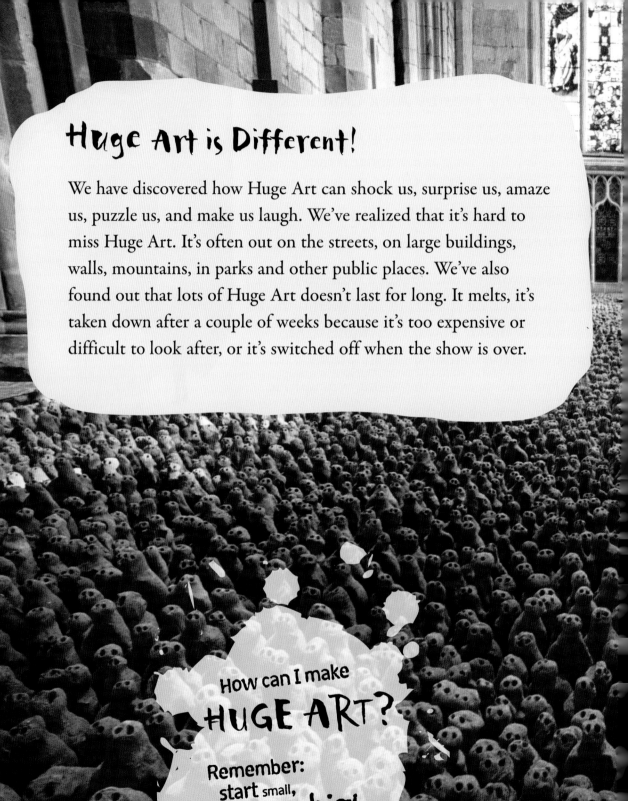

Huge Art is Different!

We have discovered how Huge Art can shock us, surprise us, amaze us, puzzle us, and make us laugh. We've realized that it's hard to miss Huge Art. It's often out on the streets, on large buildings, walls, mountains, in parks and other public places. We've also found out that lots of Huge Art doesn't last for long. It melts, it's taken down after a couple of weeks because it's too expensive or difficult to look after, or it's switched off when the show is over.

How can I make
HUGE ART?

Remember:
start small,
think big!

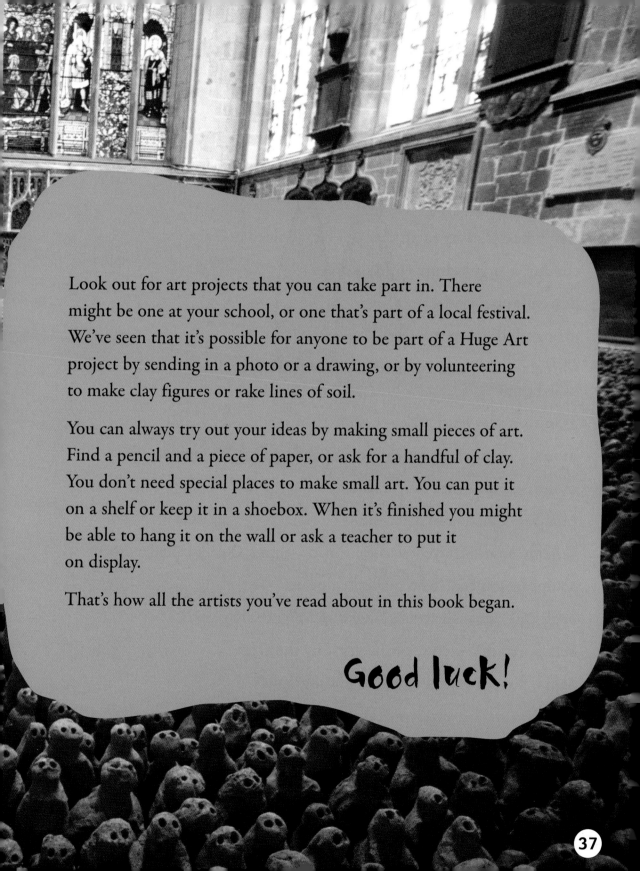

Look out for art projects that you can take part in. There might be one at your school, or one that's part of a local festival. We've seen that it's possible for anyone to be part of a Huge Art project by sending in a photo or a drawing, or by volunteering to make clay figures or rake lines of soil.

You can always try out your ideas by making small pieces of art. Find a pencil and a piece of paper, or ask for a handful of clay. You don't need special places to make small art. You can put it on a shelf or keep it in a shoebox. When it's finished you might be able to hang it on the wall or ask a teacher to put it on display.

That's how all the artists you've read about in this book began.

Good luck!

Glossary

archaeologists: people who look for evidence of how humans lived in the past

cavalry: soldiers on horseback

ceramics: items made from baked clay

clay: a heavy, sticky earth that can be moulded and shaped

condor: a large vulture (bird of prey)

descendants: relatives

dismantled: taken to pieces

fibreglass: a strong, light material made from glass and a sticky substance called resin

granite: a very hard rock

moulds: shapes into which clay or wax is pressed to harden

mounts: horses that can be ridden

portrait: a picture of a person

saffron: an orange-yellow colour made from a flower called a crocus

sculptor: someone who makes sculpture

sculpture: art made by carving, moulding or shaping

self-portrait: a picture of the artist by the artist

sepia: the brown colour of old photographs

stainless steel: a silvery metal that does not rust

terracotta: fired clay that is often a reddish-brown colour

volunteers: people who offer to do something

Index

About the Author

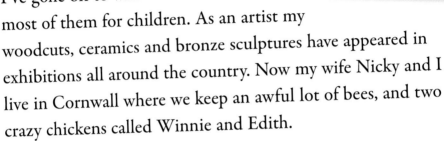

When I was at school I knew just what I wanted to be: an author, an artist and a farmer. It's taken some time, but I've finally managed all three! The first bits of writing I had published were articles in magazines. I've gone on to write more than 20 books, most of them for children. As an artist my woodcuts, ceramics and bronze sculptures have appeared in exhibitions all around the country. Now my wife Nicky and I live in Cornwall where we keep an awful lot of bees, and two crazy chickens called Winnie and Edith.

Writing this book was a voyage of discovery for me. All the art I make is very small. All the art in these pages is enormous!

Greg Foot, Series Editor

I've loved science ever since the day I took my papier mâché volcano into school. I filled it with far too much baking powder, vinegar and red food colouring, and WHOOSH! I covered the classroom ceiling in red goo. Now I've got the best job in the world: I present TV shows for the BBC, answer kids' science questions on YouTube, and make huge explosions on stage at festivals!

Working on TreeTops inFact has been great fun. There are so many brilliant books, and guess what ... they're all packed full of awesome facts! What's your favourite?